Mothering

through the Whirlwind

Other titles by
Tamara Passey

The Christmas Tree Keeper: A Novel

Mothering through the Whirlwind

TAMARA PASSEY

Winter Street Press

Winter Street Press
winterstreetpress@gmail.com

Cover design by Novak Illustration 2015

Library of Congress Control Number: 2015905245

ISBN-13: 978-0-9909840-1-6
1. Motherhood 2. Motherhood—Facing adversity

for Mom,
for leading the way

CONTENTS

ACKNOWLEDGMENTS

Thank you to the phenomenal team at Eschler Editing for their expertise in helping this book become a reality. I offer gratitude (and lots of chocolate) to my critique partners and allies in the whirlwind, Peggy and Valerie. To generous beta readers for their valuable insights: Anika, Kristin, Mari, Valerie, Elaine, and Peggy. And to my husband, who I cannot thank enough for his unfailing support.

Special thanks to the remarkable women of American Mothers, Inc., for their leadership, friendship and love.

Also, I recognize who I am today as a mother has much to do with the family and friends that have cared for and influenced me over the years. My mother, mother-in-law, sisters and sisters-in-law, and many friends—thank you for your examples of selfless love and courage. I have needed every one of them.

INTRODUCTIONS

"Don't let the whirlwinds drag you down."[1] This quote has been pinned to the corkboard in my office space since the moment I heard it. It so efficiently sums up what I've been trying to do for the last twenty-plus years as a mother. If there was any one analogy that could put into context what it was like to be setting up a crib one day and in the hospital with a sick newborn the next, it was that of a tornado—picking me up and dropping me right where I never expected to be.

Still, I have loved being a mother—not that I think I'm particularly good at it, and certainly not because it has come easy. Mothering has demanded my very best—every single day. But I love it, because I love them: my children, whom I have tried to teach and care for and coach, only to find that I have learned and gained so much more in return as we have weathered storms together.

---

1. Neil L. Anderson, "Spiritual Whirlwinds," Ensign, May 2014, 21

What kind of storms? Illness and recovery, loss of a loved one and the aftermath, relapse and relearning. My storms may be similar to or different from the storms other families face. But the parts are there. Some are predicted. Others are completely unexpected, and you find yourself riding them out or hunkering down or simply trying to brave the elements. Some storms blow over; others wreak incredible damage, no matter how prepared you might be.

When I have found myself in the middle of a whirlwind, with what I call the layers of life—layers of relationships, finances, work, health, hopes, and dreams—swirling around me, I have found plenty of advice, like, "How to talk to your teenager," but not, "How to talk to your teenager when the garage is flooded and we are out of milk." I've come across "Thirty hair-dos for your kindergartner," but not "One reliable hair-do you can manage on four hours of sleep." Advice is nice, but it gets complicated, doesn't it? What I have often longed for and benefitted most from is sharing person-to-person—hearing and being heard.

That is why I *didn't* write this collection of thoughts to tell other mothers how to weather their storms—my life has been too different for a one-size-fits-all or a neat how-to book. Rather, I simply wanted to share some of what I've been through. That's what mothers do for each other. It's how we lighten the burden and bear each other up. It helps us feel that we aren't alone. When gossip and judgment are set aside, sharing is what truly comforts us.

So I have tried to share some of my storm-braving moments, the way I would if we were old friends and you had come over to sit for a while on the porch. We would let our children play while we talked, as if all the world was easy and quiet, until the sun dipped below the trees and we'd wind down and both admit it was time to "get back." We wouldn't have to say much more than, "C'mon kids, let's go." And we would return to our lives—a little lighter, a little stronger.

SOME (INCOMPLETE) DEFINITIONS

Mothering

Adopting; Fostering; Step-mothering; Nurturing; Guiding; Teaching; Modeling; Training; Listening; Watching; Waiting; Pacing; Praying; Reading at bedtime; Reading on planes, on trains, and in automobiles; Feeding; Grooming; Nourishing; Praising; Counseling; Listening some more; Breastfeeding; Nursing; Protecting; Requiring effort; Requiring respect; Disciplining; Empathizing; Empowering; Entreating; Endearing; Grand-mothering; Elevating; Teaching some more; Creating healthy homes; Hugging; Holding; Consoling; Comforting; Coaching; Healing; Helping; Not helping; Sleeping (Ha! Almost had you there!); Not sleeping; Learning; Loving; Caring.

Whirlwind

Loss of a Loved One; Chronic illness; Medical bills; Hospital stays; Debt; Natural disasters; Financial setbacks; Property damage; Accidents; Injuries; Job loss;

Developmental delays; Divorce; Separation; Infidelity; Lost wages; Lost keys; Lost favorite recipe; Sorrow; Depression; Anxiety; Panic; Crime; Difficult family relationships; Addiction; Disability; Abuse; Blended families; Aging parents; Medical treatments; Work pressures; Flat tires; Dead batteries; Minor traffic accidents; Major traffic accidents; Schoolyard bullies; Schoolteacher conflicts; Deadlines; Missed flights; Missed recitals; Missed opportunities; Rebellious children; Added work demands; Lawsuits; Too much work; Not enough work.

Anchors

Faith; Family; Talking; Friends; Walking; Waiting; Exercise; Naps; Reading scripture; Keeping a gratitude journal; Reading comics; Long baths; Long walks; Sports; Adventure; Crafts; Learning a language; Learning a coping skill; Breathing; Yoga; Frozen yogurt; Date nights; Starry nights; Girls' nights; Plays; Movies; Concerts; Gardens; Massage; Therapy; Worship; Music; Chocolate; Green smoothies; Prayer; Taking a day off; Taking a year off; Giving up pettiness; Savoring; Appreciating; Crying; Hugging; Hand-holding; Dreaming; Forgiving; Seeing the good; Cultivating the good; Practicing patience.

ONE

GROWING UP IN A HOSPITAL HALLWAY

SUMMER 1994

I worked full time while I was pregnant with my first child, so I didn't have much extra time to daydream about what life would be like as a new mother. But I can say this: I never imagined pushing my infant son in a stroller through a hospital hallway at midnight, complete with his IV bag hanging at the side, just to pass the time.

At six months of age, my son needed a liver transplant—he was hospitalized while we waited for a donor. I slept on a cot near his metal crib. I ate cafeteria food. I held him as many hours as I could. When I wasn't sleeping, eating, or consoling, I was praying. And I was walking the halls with him in the stroller, usually at night when the halls were empty and neither of us could sleep. I'd stroll and hum, and he'd sit propped up, watching the long corridor and glass windows go by.

Consider that the *before* picture.

Now the *after*.

About one week post-transplant, our son was eight months old and we were at the medical center in San Francisco (UCSF). We'd been moved from ICU to the recovery floor, and instead of a stroller from home, we had a little red wagon for field trips.

* * *

Time out for an optional aside: I'd been to San Francisco twice before July 1994. The first time, as a freshman in college, I had road-tripped with a friend. It was Thanksgiving, and we visited a kind family that made room for college students in search of real mashed potatoes. We ventured to the city for some sightseeing. We walked Fisherman's Wharf and Ghirardelli Square.

Was there any foreshadowing? Did I pass by UCSF? Was I even remotely aware of the transplants being attempted and completed at that time? No. Not at all.

I was mostly homesick, though not for Massachusetts. I didn't want to go back to the home of my childhood as much as I wanted to fast-forward and join the family of my future. Could it be a place of safety and belonging? Would it offer more permanence than the roommate arrangements that were lucky to last a semester?

The second time I came to the Bay area, I was on my own, and it was summer. I visited the same family. I made that trip partly to keep a promise to myself—a promise I'd made sometime around the age of twelve.

When I was twelve and some of the marriages in my extended family faltered or altogether crumbled, I walked to the park across from my house. There, on a small hill, I stood on an even smaller rock and looked back at my house; then I looked around me and into the indeterminable distance. And I promised myself a few things—one of which was that if I ever thought of marrying a boy, I'd go somewhere by myself to think. I reasoned that by being alone I would not be swayed by romance or poor judgment or strong emotion. I don't know what other girls my age were thinking, but this, in my twelve-year-old mind, was a promise to be true to myself, a promise to think for myself.

I didn't have the details worked out. I'd mostly forgotten about it until the summer of 1992, when I met a certain boy. (We'll call him Steve, since that's his name.) Lots of nights after we finished homework, he and I would watch movies at the dollar theater near campus. When the semester ended and we both moved to different places, he found me by some miracle of having a roommate who knew my co-worker who just *happened* to be talking about *me* when Steve was in the room. This is the way it worked before social media.

Once we reconnected, we dated again until we both knew how we were feeling. We had some hypothetical conversations about marriage. Then I remembered my promise. So I boarded a plane and visited that kind family. They allowed me stay for a week and do little more than sleep and eat and ponder. When I alluded to why I was there, they even gave me good decision-making advice.

But here's the thing—Steve was exactly the kind of boy I didn't think existed. I may have gone away for some objectivity, for some distance so I could stop myself from making some grave mistake, but there was no mistake to be made here. He was full of love and faith and respect. He proved to be everything I thought a boy couldn't be and more. So much more. I would soon learn the kind regard he had for me, the love and faith made manifest in a thousand unexpected considerations during the difficult days that were to come.

I didn't know all that on my retreat to Northern California in 1992. I also didn't know that in two short years, I'd be on the other side of the bridge, sleeping in a hospital room with a baby boy, my son, who would be given a second chance at life. I didn't know any of that yet. But the twelve-year-old me was satisfied that the twenty-year-old me had made the best effort to think for myself.

For the sake of simplicity, I'm leaving out everything else I did, like pray and talk to good friends and read more marriage books than should be allowed by law. But let me say I don't think any of what I did was a guarantee (which is why this isn't a "how-to" book—it's a "how-I-found-my-way" book).

And so in July 1992 I said, "Yes, I will marry you." After he asked, of course. And in November, we married. Our son was born a year and two days later.

* * *

And that brings me back to the hallway at UCSF after my son's transplant.

We were waiting now to see exactly how long it would be before we'd be discharged. The doctor had said it could be three days or three weeks—everything depended on what happened when our son started drinking the special, fortified formula again.

The first time didn't go so well. Within a day of starting the formula, his abdomen swelled up like a balloon. The doctors and nurses all indicated it was normal post-op gas or swelling. Hmm. *If you say so.*

Later that day, Steve and I were at our temporary apartment for a quick dinner. It was my turn to sleep at the hospital—not-really-sleep is a more accurate description—since Steve had slept-not-slept there the night before. There was just one problem: the last shuttle of the night never arrived, so I went back to our apartment to call a taxi. It was dark by then. Steve grabbed his overnight bag and insisted on accompanying me—without complaint. This was one of those thousand kindnesses I was talking about, this quiet determined consideration of his. He wanted to be sure I'd be safe in a dark city, sacrificing another night's sleep so I would not be alone.

As it turned out, our son couldn't sleep either. His abdomen was still distended. The doctors had, not surprisingly, maintained their diagnosis of post-op gas and/or post-op swelling, both of which it could have been. Only it wasn't. In the early hours of that sleepless night, we discovered our son's bed was soaked—and not from his diaper. The wound where his surgical drain had been was leaking profusely. The nurses called the doctors, and while we waited, Steve gave our son a priesthood blessing, a religious ordinance on which we rely for healing. By mid-morning he was taken back to the operating room.

Because it was Sunday and there were no scheduled surgeries, we were able to stay with our son a little longer before they carried him off. It meant we could visit with the nurses; it was the same sort of conversation we would have if we had been friends meeting for lunch. Except we all knew we weren't. The nurses were paid to be there.

We appreciated the privacy the empty waiting room afforded us as we sat, doing our best to resist the obvious worry. What was wrong with our baby now? What would they find? And could they fix it? The families that would have normally filled the waiting room were missing, but Sunday or not, uncertainty was still there.

We had time to get something to eat, and as we rode the elevator back to the waiting room, our son's surgeon entered the crowded elevator, fresh from surgery. Was there protocol for debriefing family members in an elevator? Frankly, I didn't care. Were we going to stare at the numbers like we didn't know each other and wait until we walked to a little room with a table and a lamp and a box of tissues? No.

He told us the problem was something he usually couldn't fix. But he was pretty sure he'd fixed it. "I even bet a six-pack of beer on it," he said with a gleam in his eye. (My husband doesn't remember this comment, but we both remember the doctor *was* confident that the surgery went well.) When our son started drinking formula again, the surgeon explained, either the swelling would return and we'd be in the hospital three more weeks to allow him to heal, or he'd be fine and we could go home in three days.

Another twenty-four hours of wait-and-see. It's the way of hospital life.

To prevent myself from contemplating the abyss of *three more weeks*, I chose to think instead of Steve's kindness in the sea of uncertainty, his companionship on the rollercoaster of day-running-into-night-running-into-day. Neither of us could have known what was in store that night he chose to come with me.

But he came. And he held my hand, as he often did. And we faced it together.

Kindnesses are small things, like seeds. We mortals plant them in our meek and lowly ways. And then heaven waters them, and miracles bloom. Who can say too much of kindness?

I haven't forgotten I was telling you about this moment in the hallway:

Our son, in a red wagon. His body was no longer yellow with jaundice, but pink. The healthy glow returned right before our eyes after his transplant, like a photo developing in a dark room. A healthier little body emerged from the murky sea of cords and incisions and medications. He had more energy—both a blessing and a challenge. Hospital rooms aren't the most fun for eight-month-old babies. Hence, the hallway field trips.

On our outings, I noticed a two-year-old African-American boy. His eyes were bright yellow, his tummy bloated. I most often saw him in a wagon at the nurse's station. I finally asked the social worker about him. Her answer went something like this: "Oh, he is waiting for a transplant but will probably never receive a donor."

I couldn't have been very good at hiding my concern. "Why?" I asked.

"His parents dropped him off here when he became sick and said, in effect, 'Call us when he is better.'"

I knew this, didn't I? I knew that parents through the ages have abandoned their children in myriad ways, for reasons tragic and heartbreaking. But to see it manifest this way sickened my heart, almost unbearably. Even then, I still didn't fully understand.

"But why won't he be likely to have a transplant?"

The social worker explained, "Without a dedicated caregiver, he'd be at high-risk for transplant failure."

One sentence. A death sentence, really. What baby isn't at high-risk for all kinds of failure without a dedicated caregiver? But it's especially true for transplant kids. Our son required fourteen different medications a day, all to be dispensed at the right time and in the right amount. That was in addition to blood draws and doctor visits and daily blood pressure monitoring. Not to mention eating, diaper-changing, and bedtime stories. If *dedicated* had an over-achieving, workaholic cousin, this post-transplant caregiver would be it.

I looked into the sweet but sickly face of that little boy, his eyes full of bewilderment and pain. I could feel the longing well up inside me. Life in all its miraculous beauty and horrific injustice swirled through me, changing me. As if my own son's life-threatening illness hadn't already changed me—as if praying and waiting for a donor hadn't wrought upon my heart and softened it, fashioned it into something pliable and yielding—this abandoned little boy opened my eyes wide to love. So I could see more clearly—undeniably—what love is and what it isn't. Love is not some agreement of convenience. It is extending oneself to give life to another person, to sustain that life and foster their growth. To thrill at their success. To be there.

That had been my plan all along: to *be there* for my children. And now, the memory of that little boy in the hospital hallway meant I had no apologies and no regrets.

* * *

Our son drank his formula. I'm not sure, but I may have held my breath for two days. The swelling did not return. On the third day, we walked out through the hospital doors—crowded, bustling, splendid doors. Relieved, liberated even, we didn't look back. There was no temptation in that moment, as there could have been, to feel anything other than elation.

Maybe we should have felt nervous. But no—we soaked in what sun filtered through the layer of fog and found our way to our next temporary home.

An hour inland, we settled into Steve's grandparents' extra bedroom. Our son was in a travel crib not very far from us, his tackle box of medications near my nightstand. I crawled into bed, bone-weary tired, but triumphant. Like a new mother the night after she's given birth. Once I thought about it, our son was nearing nine months old and he'd just been given a second birth. He could live his life now.

He *would* live his life. I felt that in my bones too.

There was something else stirring inside me. A feeling of awe and humility, the feeling of an answered prayer. Or many answered prayers. I marveled at the miracle of perfect timing, of a skilled surgeon and team. The miracle of all the centers where he could have had his transplant, he was able to have it at the hospital within an hour of Steve's grandparents' home. My mind raced to record the miracles in my memory. Yet the more I tried to catalog the events, I began to sense how limited I was, even with the front-row seat to my son's life, I couldn't account for the *how* of all of it. I sensed instead, how God's power—wide and limitless—was like his love, both personal and tender.

He had orchestrated every last detail needed to provide my son a new liver, and at the same time, supplied me with a new heart.

* * *

I do not know why some moments remain in my memory more vividly and with greater impact than others. Why, for example, do I remember trying to open the chocolate milk carton in grade school, determined not to ask the aide for help? Or why does the green smell of cut grass take me to the summer when I was ten years old, barefoot, and eating strawberries from the garden? And why is it that the soft smell of rain used to mean hurried walks to school but now conjures up a white wedding dress and hurried pictures instead? Memory is a fickle friend, a benevolent companion on some days and a sly trickster on others.

That is why I have no explanation for the Mother's Day memory that has endured almost twenty years as one of my most treasured. I don't want to build it up and disappoint. It is the simplest of memories.

Mother's Day afternoon, my son and I took a short walk around the block. He was three. I was twenty-four. The day was sunny but not too hot. I don't remember what we talked about, only that we did. I remember little else about this walk, except the emotions I felt, deep and stirring. Though somewhat uneventful and ordinary, I still felt blessed and blissful. It was the kind of walk I longed for when he was in the hospital. There were no IVs and no newly ordered tests—just the trees and the sidewalk and us. His health was stable—no rejection. He was eating his vegetables and playing with friends. My biggest worry was potty training—a gloriously normal worry.

And that perhaps explains why the deepest gratitude filled me to overflowing. Of course I'd been grateful before this day, but the stress and strain of the previous three years had been consuming. Finally, I felt it—this gratitude simply to be a mother, my son's mother. And gratitude for the privilege to walk with him for however long I'd be allowed.

That's it. Not an overly impressive memory, I admit. But like I said, it has stayed with me through the years. On some stressful days, when elements of one storm or another threaten to batter me, I think on that memory, and the gratitude flows through me again.

TWO

NO ONE NEEDS ADVICE FROM A YOUNG MOTHER OF THE YEAR

JANUARY 2013

rizona Young Mother of the Year. I didn't know there was such a thing. Yet, I was that person in 2013. Mostly people wanted to know, *Why you?* They asked, "What did you have to do for that?" Or, as better stated in the alarmed worry of one of my teenagers, "How did *that* happen?"

I didn't even know how it happened. I'd agreed to be nominated; that was all. This sweet friend called and asked so thoughtfully if she could nominate me. She couldn't have known how hard the year had been—I had been coping with the health challenges of my children, my parents, and some of my own.

Learning that American Mothers, Inc., was a nonprofit service organization, I wasn't sure I could add one more thing to my plate if I was selected. But she told me other moms would be nominated as well. I relied on that, fully expecting to cheer on someone else as

Arizona's Young Mother of the Year.

My interview as a potential Young Mother of the Year fell on the same day as my daughter's birthday party. I hurried to and from the panel interview and then corralled and entertained a house full of energetic seven-year-olds. When I received the call notifying me I'd been selected, I walked my way into the laundry room for privacy, closed the door, and stared at the back of my laundry detergent for answers.

Me.

They selected me. Humbled and bewildered, all I could think was *now what?*

I knew it meant an honorary dinner, a speech, and a trip to the national convention in New York City. I knew it meant an uncomfortable spotlight on my children and me. But I also wondered if I would need to dispense any *advice.*

Not that advice is such a bad thing. It is helpful every now and then.

But I can be immersed in how-tos and should-dos, and what is it doing for me really?

Am I any less busy? Less stressed?

As a mother, what do I need the most? I ask myself this, and a dozen answers rush to be number-one on my list: More than five hours of sleep in any single night? Yes. An extra two hours in the day? Sure. But one answer starts to bubble up to the top. Listening to my intuition—I use it for finding my favorite jeans on sale, or pulling the brownies out of the oven at the right moment—but I realized that if I tuned into it instead of the Food Network, I might hear what I need: that it's okay to accept my children's shortcomings and celebrate their victories instead. That it's time to stop complaining, to no one in particular, about how my feet are a half size larger since my last pregnancy. Or that it's time to let go of what is truly weighing me down—last night's ice cream, last year's oversized purse that could swallow Shamu, or maybe the grudge I am still holding against the labor and delivery nurse for her unrepeatable comment about my breathing technique.

When I listen to that truth, I have a couple of choices. I could watch a rerun of my favorite TV show and forget anything that might lead to greater peace and happiness, or I could walk into my kitchen or bedroom or bathroom and utter a prayer—one of gratitude for the insight and another one of supplication for some willpower and mostly grace to follow through with the change.

That brings me to love. Mothers need more of it. I, we, need to be more loving.

Yes, I just wrote that. And someone is putting down this book because she is all loved out. She has given it her all and then some—and you know what? Her teenager just drove the car through the wall in the garage, after midnight. And she is saying, "Don't tell me I need to be more loving."

Telling most mothers they need to be more loving is like advising the rain to be wetter or pine trees to be more green. Most mothers have the love thing down; after all, it's an innate feminine trait that flows through their veins like estrogen or chocolate. Right? Well, I'm not so sure. Love may or may not come naturally to mothers. That's the hard truth.

But that isn't even my point.

I (we) need to be more loving in some specific ways. I need to adopt respect and integrity as a way of life. And, at a minimum, I need to demonstrate short bursts of unconditional love—until I gain stamina and can, like conditioning for a marathon, run the entire race without stopping to criticize and fix my kids.

I need to practice self-respect and self-care. Not a day at the spa, though spas do serve a purpose. I'm referring to the kind of respect I give myself when I eat right and exercise. Or the kind of respect I give myself when I call the doctor back and ask the question I was too intimidated to ask in the office.

Why do I need this as a mother? I can't give it, teach it, or model it for my children if I'm not living it myself, can I? Every self-respecting mother I know is better able to love her children with joy. The moms who don't respect themselves enough—for example, moms who don't eat their dinner warm with the rest of the family— miss out on the joy, because at some point the martyr in them can't keep up the happy act.

Integrity fits with this pattern of setting an example of self-respect. It is being able to say to my children, do as I do *and* as I say. Or it is having to say very little to my child because my actions preached the sermon for me. The kind of integrity a mother needs isn't just the dedication to telling the truth—though that is necessary. It is the ability to fulfill the assignments she takes on, not out of some superwoman complex, but because she knows her limits and accepts only those projects and assignments she can realistically accomplish. Integrity is saying yes on some days and no on others.

Integrity isn't merely living virtuously and having a noble character—it is living a whole life, or living life wholly or fully or enthusiastically. We mothers need enthusiasm for our lives that stems from respect and integrity and love because, let's face it, if our enthusiasm stems from acquiring more things to impress others or from wearing the latest fashions or from the return on our investments, we won't be believable, no matter how many acting classes we took in high school. We won't be able to ask our kids to care about kindness or the Ten Commandments; we won't be able to expect them to not ridicule their math teacher's chinos without sounding hollow ourselves. Our kids will see through our act like the paper-thin T-shirts they peddle for clothing nowadays.

One more thing about respect, integrity, and love: A mother needs the kind of self-love that involves taking a serious look at herself. Not the kind where she decides it's time to start Botox treatments—the kind where she admits her mistakes and resolves to do better.

I'm not suggesting mothers need repentance because they are awful sinners. Quite the contrary: Most mothers I know are consumed enough by the demands of family life that there is little time or room to get into real trouble. But last time I checked, mothers were not a protected class. Temptations, weaknesses, and vices are equal-opportunity visitors to women of all shapes, sizes, and mothering abilities. And, sadly, some mothers can even be more vulnerable to them because of all the demands they are constantly under.

If there is any one type of love that a mother needs, it is this: admitting a wrongdoing, making amends, and working to make it right. A mother who is doing that in her life will have what she needs to be a good mother. To say it in as few words as possible: she'll have a soft heart. She will be the soft place to land, as some have so aptly said about home and mothers. Souls that repent are kindlier and calmer, more patient, more loving. Why? Because the more often and earnestly we seek grace from heaven, the more inclined we are to offer it to everyone we meet, even our toddlers and teenagers.

* * *

I had only three minutes—the amount of time for speeches at the American Mothers convention in New York City. I couldn't find a way to say everything I wanted to in my speech—how I'd come to be there and what it meant to me and what I thought mothers could be. There was too much emotion, not enough time. I didn't sleep much the night before. I paced the bathroom floor (short paces), wondering again what I could have done to have gotten myself into a fix like this.

So instead of trying to say all of that and risk going over time, I stood the next morning for my speech in a room full of dedicated mothers and told them about the boy in the hospital hallway. About the words *dedicated caregiver*, and their impact on me.

By the nod of their heads, I knew that they already understood what I had learned—that I—and all mothers—had been given a sacred trust.

THREE

THREE THINGS *ANTIQUES ROADSHOW* TAUGHT ME ABOUT MOTHERING

DECEMBER 2010

First, know my value.

I'd seen the show before. Some homeowner finds a painting in the attic, or a teapot in the garage, and wonders if it has any value. She waits in line to talk to an expert who can evaluate what the "antique" is worth—or at least what it might sell for at auction. The thrill is when the lamp is a Tiffany or the painting is an original Monet—what are the chances? The owner is delighted and admits that it had been stashed in a corner, maybe with last year's preschool art projects piled on top of it. But now—now that she knows the item is worth tens of thousands of dollars, she eagerly agrees to go home and display it in a place of honor.

But this time I was watching the show in an attempt to take my mind off my current situation—that of another post-op recovery—and I had a different drama unfold before me. Namely, my own. See, an emergency appendectomy ten days before Christmas hadn't been part of my holiday plan. Recovery meant time in bed and no driving for six weeks, not to mention taking it easy on the bending and lifting. Did I mention Christmas was in ten days? If there was ever a season inconvenient to convalescing, this was it. Worst of all were the feelings of being an inadequate mom.

Enter *Antiques Roadshow.*

Somewhere between the Tang Dynasty marble lion that brought tears to the appraiser's eyes and the $60,000 Eskimo hunting helmet someone snagged at a flea market, I started to see a pattern.

I'd been lumping myself together with the laundry pile and last month's junk mail—and why wouldn't I, when I felt as equally unmovable and unproductive? I wasn't exactly a *bad* mom, but I felt like I was an *ineffective* mom. I knew I loved my children, but I couldn't *do* anything, could I? And if temporary disability didn't affect my self-appraisal, then surely the healthy-mom routine could. What's to value with cheerios stuck in my hair? How important can I feel when a child is kicking my shins while I try to dress her in anything other than last year's Halloween costume?

It wasn't just me. Society at large isn't any more helpful. Since the time I became a mother, the message from television shows, magazines, and Hollywood movies morphed from, "Women can have it all," (which was never true in the first place) to, "Women should try to have it all; otherwise they aren't ambitious, modern, or intelligent, or worse—they are sending their daughters the wrong message." Rarely have I seen media messages even hint, much less portray, mothers for what they are: indispensable, vital, not to mention *strong.*

Here is where I imagined for a moment if the next item up for appraisal on *Antiques Roadshow* was a mom.

This is a TAMARA PASSEY original. She has a wonderful New England influence from the Seventies. Notice the fine smile lines—evidence of the happiness she radiates to those around her. It looks like she's in decent condition, indicating the amount of dedication she's demonstrated to family and friends. What we know about this MOTHER is that she possesses listening abilities not readily seen by the untrained eye. Her value: priceless.

Second, be my authentic self.

In other words, copies are never as good as the original.

I can readily recognize the disappointment in the owner's eyes when he learns his hoped-for-masterpiece is a copy, an imitation. This concept is easily understood in art. Though some imitations and copies can fetch handsome sums, the place and value of the original is unparalleled. It is almost hard to watch the expert gently explain to the owner that his piece is worth far less than he had hoped solely because it was not the work of a master but was instead a cheaper copy.

Is it possible that I experience similar disappointment when I spend enormous amounts of energy and time trying to be as good as, or better than, someone else? I become much more confident when I spend half as much effort on being my best self, sharing the gifts and talents only I can give. My love is more authentic. It's not forced or frustrating.

Third, love accordingly.

I see myself heading back home, vowing to take better care of *me*, the MOTHER, vowing to provide her a place of honor. No question about it: I take better care of myself when I know my value. I eat nutritiously; I exercise without berating myself. I allow myself to take breaks for reading or baths, because I know I need the rejuvenation.

Does that really make me a better mother? Maybe not any single one of those things, but added together, yes, they do.

When I know how valuable my work is as mother, I take care of myself. I am a healthier woman—and a happier, better mother.

FOUR

AP ART HISTORY, DRIVER'S ED, AND GETTING OUT OF MY OWN WAY

JANUARY 2014

There stands in the Phoenix Art Museum an exquisite sculpture of two Native American figures. One is a young boy having just released an arrow to the sky. The other is an older man crouching behind him. Both of their lines of vision are fixed on the same unseen point in the distance.

The nameplate reads: *The Sun Vow*, by MacNeil, 1899.

At first I think that the sculpture doesn't have much to do with me, but I am fascinated by it.

I am chaperoning an AP art history field trip. Not that the honors students need supervision—my group triggered the alarm only once, and that was purely an accident. Thankfully, I was not the one who edged too close to the jade collection in the Asian room; but I very well could have, and my sophomore daughter would have flipped her hair and shot me a fiery glance. But I wasn't the one, and I received no reprimanding looks.

This trip was pleasant, the reward of field trips. I had graduated from the headache-inducing first- and second-grade outings, where true chaperoning—think *corralling*—was the norm.

No, today we were taking a leisurely look at *The Sun Vow.* At first glance it appeared like a grandfather teaching a young brave how to shoot an arrow. But not so. MacNeil decided to capture the rite of passage where a brave is given the opportunity to shoot an arrow into the face of the sun. The chief watches the arrow. If it disappears into the blinding glare of the sun, the brave succeeds. And if the brave succeeds, he is declared a warrior.

This clever artist captured the moment when the arrow is released and two sets of eyes—one seasoned, the other expectant—are riveted on it. I am captivated by this masterful sculpture. I follow the trajectory and want to look, too, into the sun that hangs in their sky. I am hoping to find the arrow, only not find it.

MacNeil sculpted coming of age. He sculpted the moment in our lives when we offer to the world our best, skilled effort and then wait for admittance to rule and defend that world. He sculpted the best dissertation on how to be the mother of a teenager I have yet found.

Get out of the way, or risk injury.

Take your place of support close to—but not in front of—your child-becoming-an-adult. The posture of the chief, so grand and mighty and strong, bends and folds to fit perfectly beside and behind the brave. His strength is not diminished. His importance is not any less potent. He has simply shifted his place in the sun for the boy of the rising generation to take his. He must if the tribe is to survive.

We board the bus hours later. My daughter and I chatter about the exhibits she liked; soon we stop talking and let the hum of the wheels be enough. I am thankful she is a sophomore and not a second-grader; otherwise, the bus would be deafening, and I'd be wishing for earplugs. But I am not wishing for earplugs. I am hoping to always remember *The Sun Vow.*

I especially want to remember it now, as my daughter is learning how to drive. For all our hours of driving together, I think there are so many life parallels for her to learn.

You have to know where you are going so you can be in the right lane to get there.

Construction zones, like times of intense growth or change, require a reduced speed.

Be courteous to other drivers, even if they are not.

Looking and listening can prevent a multitude of disasters.

Check your gas gauge. Don't wait until you're running on fumes. Fuel up when the tank is half-empty.

And so on.

I think I'm teaching her. But I know some lessons will take more life experience before she can appreciate them and that she must learn others on her own. But I am still so teaching-focused that I fail to recognize that *I* might have something to learn—that there might be a life lesson or two from the passenger seat for me.

Until *The Sun Vow.*

The next time we go driving I hope I remember to move over. Not just physically, but symbolically. I don't need to crouch; simply sitting in the passenger seat will be enough. She won't be shooting arrows but, rather, driving the family van.

My position as mother need not be less important, only less prominent. She will learn to drive—along with all the other survival skills she'll need to learn—better if I can remember to move out of the way.

FIVE

PLAYGROUNDS AND PRISON

2002–2005

My daughter ran from swing to slide on the playground while I sat on a bench in the sun watching her and allowing myself to heal from a recent surgery. I watched her energetic smile. She'd call from the top of the slide, "Mama, watch me!"

My cell phone rang. It was another phone call from the detective investigating my brother's murder. He had new information—a break in the case.

Two eye witnesses in the parking lot that night said they saw three men fight with my brother. At first, they saw one man fighting with my brother; then they saw a friend jump in to help. Finally, they watched a third man join in the beating. Once my brother was on the ground, they kicked him and trampled him. With their boots.

The man on the phone gave me the details carefully. He didn't dwell on the attack but instead focused on what they were doing to find the men, if they could be identified, and how great it was to have eyewitnesses.

I sat on the bench, motionless, yet reeling. Mere minutes of a call with *great* news, and the images returned. Finally we had answers to explain the blood on the ground. We had numbers—three to one—to explain why he couldn't defend himself, something a 6-foot, 170-pound, 37-year-old man could have easily done had it been against one man, or even two. But not three.

The new information may have answered some questions, but it had created new ones, too. Did the witnesses try to do anything? Could they see who had started the fight? Did it matter? And there still wasn't any clue about *why*. Why did these men do what they did? Did they even have a reason?

"Watch this!" My daughter shouted. I gripped the edge of the metal bench and focused on her tiny frame climbing up a ladder under sunny skies. She was innocent and carefree—blissfully unaware of the ugly, awful capacity of man. Monsters in her imaginary world had fuzzy blue hair, names like "Sully," and were afraid of children.

Monsters in the real world were men who gave themselves over to unrestrained and wild rage, like they were putting out a fire—stomping until there was nothing but the faintest dying embers. Were they ever four years old? Did they ever play on the swings and run and play tag? What happens in a boy's life—or a man's life—to make him so he can do such things?

I didn't want to know.

* * *

In a jail cell, two thousand miles from my life, sits the man who killed my brother.

That could have been the first line of the next

chapter. But the jury found the man not guilty. I wouldn't have minded their verdict so much if they could have also found my brother *not dead*. But he *is* dead—ever since the day in the hospital when his body quit living and my father had to lift my mother's wailing body off of him. My sister witnessed the entire dreadful scene, complete with nurses behind the next curtain talking and laughing and, you know—just *living*.

"I wanted to say something to those nurses," my sister recounted to me an hour later in the airport, "but I knew it didn't matter. They work there, and people die there all the time."

Technically he died there. That is what it says on the death certificate that we had to have ten copies of for the life insurance company. It makes no mention that he mostly died on the ground a week earlier. Any trace of him—his sense of humor, his smile, his strength—were gone by the time my father was called to identify the body. *What was left of the body.* His face so swollen my father had to look at the pants he wore to confirm my mother's lifelong nightmare: their son had been beaten and left for dead in a parking lot. Now somewhere on the streets were the men who did it, including the man who was arrested and sat three years in jail, awaiting trial.

Three years we waited for the trial. Three years the man sat in a jail cell on the East Coast, while I lived my life on the West. During those years, a little daydream formed in my mind. I replayed it at various intervals while living my life as a mom of two young children.

It went something like this: I'd drive to the jailhouse, park, and walk slowly to the doors. I'd soak in the sun I knew the prisoner could not enjoy. I'd breathe deeply the fresh air of freedom I knew he didn't have. I would walk through the security checkpoints and hear the lock of doors behind me. I could see the dingy walls and even smell the staleness. I'd walk into the room and take my seat across the table from the man, the man who did not stop kicking.

Here is where I'd interview him. There were always different questions. "Why did you do it? And how could you? Did you even know who you were killing?" And then I'd practice looking him squarely in the eye and saying, "I forgive you." Then *I* would get up and leave.

Only the jury, the citizens of my hometown who reported for jury duty in the middle of whatever else they wanted to be doing, had to listen and decide the fate of this man. The jury found him not guilty. If it sounds like I'm repeating myself, yes, some days it's like that.

The moment I learned the verdict—I happened to be looking for maternity clothes at JC Penney at the time—it was as if someone else was directing my daydream. The newly found-not-guilty man stood and shed his prisoner's costume. And he walked away without even looking back. *I* was the one who sat in the chair, looking at the dingy walls and locked doors.

What of the answers to my questions? What of my words *I forgive you*? They were easy to say to a man who I thought was living in jail, somehow paying for his crime. But now? I was kidding myself, wasn't I? All my efforts to extend forgiveness were now exposed for what they were: conditional. And with that, they became hollow and empty, just like my make-believe jail room.

I wanted to protest, to pound the table, to demand an appeal. I wanted to cry quietly by myself for the injustice of it all. No matter how I tried to redirect the ending of the daydream, it was me, always me, sitting there alone in my imagined cell—my heart aching for answers one minute and hardening for lack of answers in the next. I felt twisted inside out, drained of the ready love I'd had all my life for family and friends and my children.

My children. The playground. *Let's go to the park, Mama*, they would ask. And I would take them, and I would try to pull my thoughts away. And that is when it hit me. An unforgiving heart is an imprisoned one.

Gradually, I no longer needed the daydream. I had my own life to live. I had sunshine and squeals. I could sit and breathe and heal, not only from surgery but from unseen wounds. Maybe my children created some of the whirlwinds I had to learn to navigate; but in some storms, at least this raging storm, my children were an unexpected anchor.

SIX

WHAT I LOST AND FOUND IN THE DOCTOR'S WAITING ROOM

A funny thing happens when you troll your memory for details: It can produce all kinds of irrelevant material. Or maybe this just occurs to me. I try to remember a doctor's name, and all I can see is the painting in his waiting room. Or I try to remember how old my child was during a certain procedure, and my memory serves up the color of the curtains in the hospital or the L-shape of its hallway.

I'd been planning on writing a different chapter here. A postscript of sorts. But that would have been a bit false. I'm still mothering in the whirlwind; there is nothing *post* about it.

Despite my best efforts to piece together some paragraphs to sum up all these experiences, my mind has returned to a theme of doctor visits instead. That's not too surprising, considering how many I've gone through during my mothering career. And sure, there are numerous analogies available—needing medical attention and advice, seeking healing and hope. But those analogies are not what my mind has been mulling over.

Going to the doctor was an inescapable part of my role as mother. I didn't question it. I didn't even notice for the first handful of years, if that makes sense. Eventually, I allowed myself to think about my friends and their healthy children and how, in their lives, the doctor wasn't visited like a family friend. I began to joke to myself—*what is my life but a doctor's waiting room?*

But I knew why I was there and what I was doing. And I was okay.

Mapping, driving, arriving, signing in, paying co-pays, weighing, discussing, prescribing, wrangling with the insurance company (at least we had insurance, right?), scheduling follow-up appointments—it was all as routine as trips to the grocery store.

Until the restlessness crept in.

The impatient years were filled with me trying to *do* something in those intolerable minutes in the waiting room chairs. Read, write, anything that felt more meaningful than waiting. I took up Sudoku. Brain health, right?

I might have overcome the impatience and moved on to acceptance if the normal ebb and flow of health and visits had continued as it had in the past. But like rain and bumper crops, there were a few years that yielded a record number of visits for my children and their various health needs—some routine, some serious. And then my health needed attention. More visits. About this time a friend remarked in an innocent, offhand way, "Gee, I haven't set foot in a doctor's office in more than a year, and you are going to a different place every week."

Cue the whirlwind of resentment. Cue the frustration over feeling resentment.

One minute I'm enjoying my life—all of it, both the joy and the difficulty. And then *whoosh*. The next minute I'm snatched up and plunked down in the middle of a conflicted mess of emotions.

I didn't feel sorry for myself, and I surely didn't want anyone else feeling sorry for me. Maybe I didn't have control over all the needs of my children, but I accepted the demands of being their mother with all of the blessings that came with it—a package deal. *A sacred trust.* That's why I avoided comparisons to other mothers the same way I avoided potholes and dead ends. I also refused to count the cost. I specifically didn't want to add up hours that would surely amount to days, even years of my life given over to managing the care of my children. I loved them. I would do it all again, no questions asked. *Time well spent* had been my refrain.

So why was I feeling resentful?

I had resisted thoughts about what I'd lost, but they washed over me anyway. What had I lost? What other things could I have spent my time doing? Anything else. Earning degrees. Earning money. Learning to paint. Learning to rock climb. Did I even know what I would have done with the time? Did it matter? Was I kidding myself? Wouldn't I have just been at home anyway, doing more dishes, doing more laundry?

Oh, resentment is a canker and a curse. It spreads like weeds and chokes the life out of any happy goodness. I'd given my life to what? What did I have to show for it? No stamps in a passport, no postcards of yet another nondescript wall of office art. *How did this happen?* I wondered. *How did I lose my life like this?*

These were not easy thoughts. Not enjoyable feelings. I didn't talk about them or even write about them, but I did puzzle over them. They weren't chronic; they were more like sporadic feelings of resentment, cropping up when life became overly busy or when I truly had other things I wanted to do. *What is this feeling?* I wondered. *Why does this feel like a grand imposition now?*

And more than any other emotion, I felt disheartened over it. *Is this what I'm becoming? Cranky and stingy with my time?* This was the opposite of the mother I wanted to become—the mother I thought I was becoming.

And I didn't seem to have an antidote.

Until one day—until another doctor visit. This time, my son was now an adult and I was an invited guest. He no longer needed me to sign forms or even be part of the conversation. But I was there because these were serious discussions over test results and the doctor was giving my son a choice of what treatment option he wanted.

This doctor had a soft-spoken voice, intelligent and clear. His voice also had an accent that gave his words a lilt, a subtle emphasis in unexpected places.

After explaining my son's options, the doctor said, "If this is what you choose, I will walk this path with you."

A quiet moment ensued while thoughtfulness filled the square exam room. My son sat, contemplating the consequences of his choice, and the doctor waited to learn which path he'd take.

And me? My life flashed before my eyes. Right there in that room.

I will walk this path with you.

With those words, I knew the doctor was describing what he'd do as my son's doctor. He would write the prescriptions, order the tests, explain the results. He'd be there.

But he was also inadvertently giving voice to the girl I'd forgotten—the fresh-faced, hope-filled, twenty-something mother I'd once been. The one who walked with her infant son through hospital hallways, the one who set out to be that dedicated caregiver.

I will walk this path with you.

We left the hospital. We walked through the lobby and out to the parking garage. My son drove home. I—the passenger—watched the hospital retreat in the rearview mirror. I marveled at the simplicity of it.

Had I complicated it so much? Had I fallen prey to media messages and cultural traditions—thinking that mothering had to be so much more glamorous, more accomplished? Had I forgotten that it was as simple as walking, watching over, and being there? Was this what my children needed—a traveling companion for this world of trial and beauty, of wonder and woe?

I climbed into bed that night, the winds of the whirlwind, now calm. The resentment had drained out of me. The memory of a Mother's Day years earlier settled in my mind.

The trees, the sidewalk, and us.

Compassion and gentleness and gratitude.

There it was, what I'd been trying to describe, trying to find in myself, in one sentence.

I will walk this path with you.

AFTERWORD

FAITH MATTERS

I cannot remember a time when I did not believe in God and in His Son Jesus Christ. This faith has been my anchor through every storm—protecting me, sheltering me. This faith has been my refuge from all the forces that would drag me down. This faith has softened my afflictions and enlarged my joys. It has given purpose to my path in a sometimes-senseless world. And it has made all the difference in my role as mother. There is no other anchor as solid and sound as the Rock of our Redeemer, the Son of God. Everything I have needed to survive the whirlwinds, and teach my children how to do the same, has been supplied in His love.

In the fourteenth chapter of John are three verses that have sustained me:

"If ye love me, keep my commandments" (John 14:15).
"I will not leave you comfortless" (John 14:18).
"Peace I leave with you, my peace I give unto you: not as the world giveth, give I unto you. Let not your heart be troubled, neither let it be afraid" (John 14:27).

I would no sooner abandon my faith during a difficult time than I would jump ship in a storm on the high seas. The mercy and grace from a loving Father in Heaven has carried me through. I have offered up my bruised and broken heart, and time after time He has returned it to me whole.

ABOUT THE AUTHOR

Tamara Passey is a mother, author, and poetry enthusiast. She was named Arizona Young Mother of the Year in 2013. Author of *The Christmas Tree Keeper: A Novel,* she also contributes marriage and family articles to FamilyShare.com. When she's not writing or switching laundry loads, she can be found walking, baking or reading—though not all at the same time. She lives with her husband and their three children in Arizona. You can find her online and read her speech given at the AMI Convention at

TamaraPassey.com

She also blogs at

FivePagesOfSomething.blogspot.com

For more information about American Mothers, Inc., visit their website:
www.americanmothers.org